MW01595296

7

KEYS

OF

DELIVERANCE

7 Keys of Deliverance © 2017 Moises Ramirez

All rights reserved. No part of this publication may be reproduced, distributed, or transmitted in any form or by any means, including photocopying, recording, or other electronic or mechanical methods, without the prior written permission of the publisher, except in the case of brief quotations embodied in critical reviews and certain other noncommercial uses permitted by copyright law.

All biblical scriptures except were noted were taken from New King James Version.

Translation: Francisco Damian
Edited: Moises E. Ramirez
Revised by: Serena Ramirez
Design: Moises E. Ramirez

ISBN: 978-1542877046

Category: Religion / Christian Ministry / Discipleship

Printed by CreateSpace, An amazon.com Company
Available on Kindle and other online stores.

7

KEYS

OF

DELIVERANCE

Apostle: Moises Ramirez

E220 Church
Ministry of Restoration,
Deliverance & Spiritual Warfare

Apostle Moises Ramirez

INDEX   5

Apostle Moises Ramirez

OBJECTIVES

— The purpose of this book "7 Keys of Deliverance" is so as many people as possible know a little more about the spiritual realm.

— So that as many people as possible have in their hands these 7 keys of liberation and put them into practice.

— So that as many people as possible experience freedom in different areas of their lives.

INTRODUCTION

Welcome to this book "7 Keys of Deliverance". In this book you will learn 7 Keys to experience freedom in different areas of your life and we'll explain how the spiritual realm of darkness works.
You will be able to work self-deliverances and also help other people that are in bondage to experience freedom in Christ.

I encourage you to know these 7 keys of deliverance that God has given to His church and put them into practice so that you may be free in all areas of your life.

Apostle Moises Ramirez

ABOUT THE AUTHOR

The Apostle Moises Ramirez is a man called by God to expand the Kingdom of Heaven here on earth through the supernatural power of God.

Christian from birth, he is the founder of the church Efesios 2:20 widely known as E220 Church in different cities in the state of Texas and Mexico.

Committed to the great commission that Jesus left us before going to heaven "GO THROUGHOUT THE WORLD AND MAKE DISCIPLES" making disciples in each of the churches established.

Within his calling he has the mission to restore and deliver those who are captive, through spiritual warfare, evangelizing, affirming, discipleship and sending each of them to do the same.

Studying in C.B.S. in Houston Texas in the area of Hispanics and more diversity of studies and courses, he is the author of the books: "MANUAL OF DELIVERANCE" and "VISION CRECE" which can also be found in Spanish.

He preaches the message that Jesus Christ brought to this earth, the message of the kingdom, having Christ as the center of all.

The Apostle Moises Ramirez resides in the city of Abilene TX with his wife Eva, son Moy, and daughter-in-law Serena, together they have established what is today a ministry of restoration, spiritual warfare and deliverance.

Apostle Moises Ramirez

ACKNOWLEDGMENTS

I thank the Lord Jesus Christ for the opportunity He gives me to share with you this book of deliverance, thanks to my beloved wife, my son and daughter-in-law for being by my side in the difficult times of my life, for knowing how to encourage me when I needed it the most, for respecting and honoring my paternity.

I thank all the disciples that God has allowed me to train in different ministries of E220 Church and all members in general for believing in me and in my calling, I love them all equally.

I thank Francisco Damian for translating this book into the English language for many more to be blessed.

To all, my biggest and most sincere thanks, I love you all in the Lord because you are part of my life.

Blessings.

Moises Ramirez

Apostle Moises Ramirez

CHAPTER I

DESIGNS

I ask God that these 7 keys will be a blessing to your life and help you every day to be more free. Pray to God and ask Him for revelation and to open your understanding before reading this book. They're 7 keys that God has left us in His word and now is the time for them to be revealed. Thanks to God and all His prophets and apostles of today who are bringing these new revelations. I must mention with respect and give due honor to the prophetess Ana Mendez for having a sensitive ear to the voice of God. I desire that God will continue to use her even more than He already has, to be a blessing to all the souls who are in captivity.

I want you to understand very well the topic of designs so that you may put it into practice in your life. The word of God says, "My people perish for lack of knowledge" (Hosea 4:6), and what I want is, through this teaching, you may acquire knowledge for your type of prayer to change. And you shall know the truth and the truth shall make you free (John 8:32), for you to be free in some areas of your life.

NATURAL REALM

The natural world operates based on designs, everything physical is created based on a previous design, it is to say, everything that you see already existed before you saw it finished.

Hebrews 11:3b "...SO THAT THE THINGS WHICH ARE SEEN WERE NOT MADE OF THINGS WHICH ARE VISIBLE"

This biblical scripture is speaking of both the natural and spiritual world, what you see, already existed before you saw it.

EXAMPLE: A building, house, car, television, or whatever you want to name, first existed in a plan named design.

An architect designs a blueprint to express how he wants a building to be built and once the design is completed he proceeds to show what is in the blueprint, then when you see the building finished you might say, "they just finished building it", but the truth is, that the building already existed in a design before you saw, the architect's mind had already visualized it long before it came into existence.

Everything in the physical and spiritual world operates on designs.

NATURAL AND SPIRITUAL WORLD

If we apply this same scripture in Hebrews, we will realize the spiritual world is more real than the natural world.

Because it says: "what is seen was made from the unseen" therefore planet earth was created from something unseen, it is to say from a spiritual world. That is why the Bible speaks of two earths.

Now let's talk about the spiritual world of darkness, warlocks, sorcerers and others who are dedicated to working in this realm.

Sorcerers know how to work with designs, the Bible says that the children of darkness are wiser than the children of light and that is true. (Luke 16:8) Unfortunately the church in terms of spiritual life is very ignorant and they're perishing.

EXAMPLE: A sorcerer grabs a rag doll aka voodoo doll and puts a name on it and begins working on it. He sticks it with needles in the head, and the person says:
— "I have a headache,"
they go to the doctor and the doctor says:
— "you have migraines,"
and prescribes pills which do not take away the pain because its not a natural illness but rather a spiritual illness, and the spiritual illness is solved through the spirit.

That's an example of a witch working with designs, but there are different types of designs. A voodoo doll, a photograph, nails, hair, saliva, blood, clothing, food dishes, etc., are used in designs to work in different ways, to provoke accidents, illnesses, divorce, to bound people together, for one to loose their mind, or even cause death.

The spiritual realm is more real than the natural world and the church has not realized it. That is why the church is paying the consequences. In the end, all these designs are natural working with the spiritual realm through a prophetic act, accompanied by a declaration. The prophetic act is when the witch sticks the needle to the voodoo doll and the declaration is what they want to happen to that person, in this case, the headache.

SPIRITUAL REALM

Isaiah 7:6 "LET US GO UP AGAINST JUDAH AND TERRORIZE IT; AND LET US BREACH ITS WALL AND TEAR IT APART EACH OF US TAKING A PORTION AND SET UP THE SON OF TABEEL OVER IT AS ITS KING,"

This scripture begins by saying: "Let us go up against Judah"

JUDAH – One of the twelve tribes of Israel, and the Bible says that the church is Israel, and the church is us, therefore, if I make this verse personal, I'm not altering the scripture.
Then it would say this: "let us go against you" or "they come against me". I'm applying this verse to your life or mine.

TERRORIZE IT – After they come against your life, they place fear. If you have been afraid in life, then this verse has been fulfilled in you.

TEAR IT APART - After they come against your life and terrorize you, they say: "let's tear it apart" Tear what apart? the answer is: your life, your soul, is torn to pieces.

How? they fragment you into pieces and each one takes its portion. If you have ever been scared or afraid, you might feel an emptiness upon your chest, your soul has been fragmented, and then phrases are spoken like "I feel my heart broken," "I feel empty inside," or "my soul is torn apart". These are phrases where your soul is telling you that it's torn.

EACH OF US TAKING A PORTION – Who is "us"? I will clarify that God will never place fear or terrorize, and much less divide a soul. Then these words can not be of God, but rather the devil. He and his demons are having a meeting and are planning the destruction of your life and he is telling his demons how they are going to do it. When he says, "each of us" it is referring to the devil and his demons.

Let us continue explaining this interesting verse and you will realize that your soul is already fragmented and needs to be set free.

AND SET UP THE SON OF TABEEL OVER IT AS ITS KING - After they go to your soul, placed fear, fragmented and divided the soul among them, they say within themselves, "we're going to put in the middle of this soul a king", what is so tremendous about this is that "Tabeel" means "*good for nothing*". This means that they set a spirit inside your soul to reign in the midst of your soul and tells you in every opportunity available that you are good for nothing. One of the devil's functions is to make you believe that you are good for nothing, for you not to progress and with that useless mindset you are spending your time thinking negatively, therefore you're not able to advise in life because your soul has been fragmented.

This is how the spiritual world works, when the devil and his demons do all their work in your soul.

They make a design in the spiritual realm to work against your life, and the more you try to go forward in life there is always something that doesn't allow you to. That is why Christians spend their time sitting in a chair, inside a church, wanting to do the will of God but are unable to. Because there is a design upon their life that does not allow them to. Their life has already been designed so that the purpose of God will never be fulfilled upon them.

Psalms 74:2-3 "REMEMBER YOUR CONGREGATION, WHICH YOU HAVE PURCHASED OF OLD, WHICH YOU HAVE REDEEMED TO BE THE TRIBE OF YOUR INHERITANCE; REMEMBER MOUNT ZION, WHERE YOU HAVE DWELT. TURN YOUR FOOTSTEPS TOWARD THE PERPETUAL RUINS; THE ENEMY HAS DAMAGED EVERYTHING WITHIN THE SANCTUARY."

Let's look at this verse and try to explain it so you can better understand it. This is a design of destruction the devil has against the temples where the word of God is preached.

Asaph the singer is telling God to remember his congregation, therefore he's talking about a congregation or church. Verse 3 says "direct your steps to the perpetual ruins", you may ask What are the perpetual ruins? They are a certain area of hell. Asaph tells God to go towards a certain part of hell to see. To see what? To see all the evil that the enemy has done in the sanctuary. Where is the evil that the devil is doing against the sanctuary? In hell.

The devil may fabricate a design to destroy your life but he also fabricates evil designs against the sanctuaries on earth he places strongholds, cancels them, forces them to close, etc. All this happens in the spiritual realm and sooner rather than later the design is carried out and that's the reason why so many temples are closing their doors.

TESTIMONY

On one recent occasion, the Lord had given us a building and a satanist visited us for two consecutive days. At first we did not suspect or discern anything but my wife noticed something odd. He was the first one to arrive at the temple, go straight to the altar, pray for the pews, and the walls of the sanctuary. On the next visit, the Holy Spirit revealed through one of the prophets everything he had done through his prayers. The prophet was able to see how pews were bound by chains, the sanctuary doors were locked with chains and padlocks. We began to destroy all of the devil's designs against the sanctuary and some spirits began to manifest in the person. The spirits through his mouth began to say that the person had five pacts with the devil, that he is a member of one of the largest Christian churches in the city and that he had been sent to destroy this church.

The devil infiltrates his disciples in all churches to stop progress and for it to be destroyed. He designs a plan of destruction for the church and if the different gifts of the Spirit of God are not activated, the church will certainly be destroyed without fulfilling the purpose of God on Earth.

HOW TO KNOW IF THERE ARE DESIGNS OF THE DEVIL IN MY LIFE

When you are struggling in an area of your life and you have already tried to solve it in several ways and nothing works for you. On the contrary, you feel that the struggle is getting worst more and more, then there is probably a design against your life. It can be a design against your health, a design of division, of divorce, of lawsuits, a design for an accident, for destruction, a design for death, etc...

UNDOING DESIGNS

It is very simple to undo the designs of the devil. You just have to learn to pray differently than you've been doing up until today. Here is an example.

PRAYER:

In the name of the Lord Jesus Christ I break, destroy, and cancel all designs the devil has against my _____, (life, husband, son, family, church, city, etc.) all designs of _____(Illness, ruin, poverty, division, death, destruction, accidents, divorces, lawsuits, etc.) I cancel it, I destroy it in the name of Jesus Christ. All prayers from a warlock, sorcerer, witch doctor, or curse launched against _____(name) by any person, relative, christian, pastor or demons, is canceled in the name of Jesus Christ. I destroy every altar built by a warlock, where they have designed the life of: _____ (name) I put out the candles, I throw the oil, holy water, salt and rescue the picture or voodoo doll with the name: _____(name of person which you are praying for) I take out the needles and remove the chains off,

I anoint it with the blood of the Lord Jesus Christ, and declare that _____(name) is set free in the name of Jesus Christ.

PROPHETIC ACTS

Lets say a fragment of your soul is in a region of captivity. We must do prophetic acts to recover the soul fragments from the region of captivity, also remember that every prophetic act is always followed by a declaration.

EXAMPLE: If a piece of your soul is in some area of hell, then you just have to bend and in a figurative way reach for your soul fragment and bring it back to your chest. You have to do it as often as necessary and with great faith. Sometimes God will allow you to see yourself descending to dark places to recover yourself, or see a cell, or dark room, or any other region of captivity.
Later we will see what Regions of Captivity are.

CONCLUSION

I hope the subject of designs to be a blessing for you and your family. Put into practice everything you have just learned and you will see the results in your life. Let this be your every day prayer, to break designs of the devil against your family and yourself.

Blessings.

Apostle Moises Ramirez

CHAPTER II

INIQUITY

What is iniquity?
1. What is twisted or has been deviated.
2. Whatever twists the original design of creation.
3. It is the seed that produces sin.

God drew an original design for everything but iniquity is responsible for twisting or diverting the design of God.

BIRTH OF INIQUITY

Ezekiel 28:16 "THROUGH THE ABUNDANCE OF YOUR COMMERCE YOU WERE FILLED WITH INIQUITY, AND YOU SINNED; THEREFORE I HAVE CAST YOU OUT FROM THE MOUNTAIN OF GOD, AND I HAVE DESTROYED YOU, FROM THE MIDST OF THE STONES OF FIRE, O COVERING CHERUB"

Here we can see where iniquity is born, God designed an original design for Lucifer and iniquity deviated him. Note, it says he was filled with iniquity and then sinned, it is

23

to say, iniquity led him to sin, therefore iniquity is the seed that produces sin.

TWO SEEDS

Genesis 3:15 "AND I WILL PUT ENMITY BETWEEN YOU AND THE WOMAN, AND BETWEEN YOUR SEED AND HER SEED; HE SHALL BRUISE YOU ON THE HEAD, AND YOU SHALL BRUISE HIM ON THE HEEL."

If we study this passage with revelation we will realize that it is talking about two seeds, the seed of the woman and the seed of the devil. For years they have taught us about the seed of the woman and know that it is Jesus, but who is the seed of the devil? We can now understand that iniquity is the seed of the devil, so wickedness is not born but rather it is transferred from generation to generation.

INIQUITY IS TRANSFERRED

Exodus 34:7 "KEEPING STEADFAST LOVE FOR THOUSANDS.
FORGIVING INIQUITY, TRANSGRESSION, AND SIN.
BUT WHO WILL BY NO MEANS CLEAR THE GUILTY.
VISITING THE INIQUITY OF THE FATHERS ON THE CHILDREN AND CHILDREN'S CHILDREN, TO THE THIRD AND FOURTH GENERATION."

Notice this is saying that God forgives iniquity, rebellion and sin, making a clear difference between iniquity and sin. For years we thought that iniquity was the same as sin, and believed that just repenting of sins was enough, but that's a mistake. So many Christians struggle for years with the same sins they had repented for many years ago, not understanding what's happening and they eventually get frustrated and end up walking away from Christ.

To repent of our sins is like cutting the fruit of a tree; it will produce fruit again next year. As long as you don't take out the tree with its roots, it will continue to give fruit. Likewise with sin, we are cutting sins by repenting, but the the seed of iniquity stays in, and the next year will produce sin again.

Verse 7 continues to say that God visits the "*iniquity*" of the fathers upon the children and grandchildren even in the third and fourth generation. He's not saying He visits the "sins" of the fathers, God is making a clear distinction between sin and iniquity, being iniquity the one transferred from generation to generation. Not the sins.

Ezekiel 18:20a "THE PERSON WHO SINS IS THE ONE WHO WILL DIE. THE CHILD WILL NOT BE PUNISHED FOR THE PARENT'S SINS, AND THE PARENT WILL NOT BE PUNISHED FOR THE CHILD'S SINS..."

It's very clear, the person who sins will give account for their own sin, the children do not have to pay the consequences for their parents' sins, nor the parents pay the consequences for the sins of their children, but, with iniquity, yes. Parents do transfer iniquity to their children.

HOW IS INIQUITY TRANSFERRED?

2 Corinthians 7:1 "THEREFORE, BELOVED, SINCE WE HAVE THESE PROMISES, LET US CLEANSE OURSELVES FROM ALL FILTHINESS OF THE FLESH AND SPIRIT, PERFECTING HOLINESS IN THE FEAR OF GOD"

Look what Paul is saying, for us to cleanse ourselves from all defilement of flesh and spirit. When we repent of our sins we are cleaning the flesh, since sin is usually in the flesh, but, what about the spirit? Paul is also saying to cleanse the spirit. If sin is in the flesh, then the iniquity is in the spirit, we have done things backwards. First we want to clean the flesh and then our inner being. If we first clean the spirit of every defilement of iniquity, we will also be cleaning our flesh.

I will try to explain in the simplest way possible to make it clear as to how iniquity is transferred.

The Bible says that the spirit of life is in the blood. The blood is produced by the bone marrow, and the bone marrow is inside the bones, therefore the spirit of life is within the bones, in other words, it is in the blood. Now, when a sperm fertilizes an egg there is a transference of iniquity from man. The sperm is blood, and to form a new baby in the womb of the mother it is fed with blood through the umbilical cord, therefore iniquity is in the blood of people.

If we have our blood contaminated with iniquity, and the blood irrigates the whole body, then we will have a body full of diseases. That is why there are so many diseases caused by contaminated blood.

INIQUITY IN HEBREW

INIQUITY = JAMAS = Violence, injustice, falsehood evil, decomposition.

If there is violence, falsehood, injustice, or evil, If there are areas in your life twisted, broken, or about to be rotten, surely there is iniquity in your life and you must repent from it.

INIQUITY IN GREEK

INIQUITY = ANOMIA = Illegality, wickedness.

Anything illegal, dirty business, embezzlement, theft, and anything evil is produced by iniquity. The word evil, or wicked is the same as iniquity, the word iniquity in many texts has been changed to evil or wickedness in the Bible, therefore, when you read the word evil or wicked in the Bible, most of the time it is referring to iniquity.

The word anemia is derived from the word *"anomia"*, which we know is a blood disease.

So we know that iniquity is transferred through the sperm from the father to the children and the grandchildren, this is what we know as generational curses. That is why the Lord Jesus said, "the devil has nothing in me." because Jesus was not begotten by an earthly father.

INIQUITY ATTRACTS CURSES

We must understand that every day curses are being released against our lives and our families. Curses of death, diseases, poverty, divorce, addictions, etc., and if there is iniquity in your life, iniquity will attract curses into your life.

For example a witch, neighbor, pastor or anyone else who speaks against you can send a curse of envy and if you have iniquity in your life; you will be impregnated within and in due time that curse will produce its fruit.

HOW TO CUT ALL INIQUITY

To be free from all iniquity; It takes a process in which you have to start rejecting, cutting, and cast out all iniquity of your life.

Prayer: All iniquity of alcoholism, addictions, sexual perversions etc, I reject you, I cut you off, and I cast you out of my life in the name of Jesus Christ.

Because iniquity is in the blood, when you are rebuking the iniquity you may have pains in the bones or in the spine cause that is usually where iniquity is found, also you may bleed through the nose, mouth, or when going to the bathroom. But please don't be alarmed, this is normal when you reject iniquity from your body.

TESTIMONY

In my case, when I started teaching the church about iniquity and ministered to cast out the iniquity, I bled through my nose, others bled through the mouth and others when they went to the bathroom. As horrific as it may sound, what is important is that we are set free from all iniquity to change our lives for good and to experience freedom in Christ.

I have to mention that iniquity manifests itself in the form of a python or viper, and gets entangled in the spine therefore many experience back pain, but all it takes is doing prophetic acts, as if you are unraveling it from your spine and casting it out and you will see the results.

CONCLUSION

To speak of iniquity is to speak of a unknown subject for many churches. I recommend that you apply these revelations that God is giving to His people so that we may be free from all iniquity.

If you want to learn more about the subject I recommend a book written by the prophetess Ana Mendez called "Iniquity". There she explains the subject of iniquity more deeply.

Blessings

Apostle Moises Ramirez

CHAPTER III

BONES

Speaking of bones in the Bible is a subject that the church should not ignore.

-It is the system that holds the entire body standing.
-The adult human has 206 bones which are given the name skeleton.
-Within the bones is the bone marrow. A fatty tissue responsible for producing blood cells.
-The blood is produced inside the bones.
-The Bible says that the spirit of life is in the blood.
-The spirit of life is inside the bones.

The devil knows all of this information, therefore he attacks humans with diseases in the blood and bones. In the spiritual realm he captures or designs a design for your bones to have them trapped and for that reason many people suffer from pains in the bones.

THE FORMATION OF WOMEN

Genesis 2:21-23 "AND THE LORD GOD CAUSED A DEEP SLEEP TO FALL ON ADAM, AND HE SLEPT; AND HE TOOK ONE OF HIS RIBS, AND CLOSED UP THE FLESH IN ITS PLACE. THEN THE RIB WHICH THE LORD GOD HAD TAKEN FROM MAN HE MADE INTO A WOMAN, AND BROUGHT HER TO THE MAN. AND ADAM SAID: THIS IS NOW BONE OF MY BONES AND THE FLESH OF MY FLESH; SHE SHALL BE CALLED WOMAN, BECAUSE SHE WAS TAKEN OUT OF MAN"

If we know the story of the creation of humanity, God created man from the dust of the earth and blew the breath of life into him, but the woman was formed from a rib. The woman was formed of a living matter, therefore He did not have the need to breathe life into her because the bone already had life.

With this we can realize that the bones for God are very important, because the spirit of life is in the bones.

THE BONES OF JOSEPH

Genesis 50:25 "THEN JOSEPH TOOK AN OATH FROM THE CHILDREN OF ISRAEL, SAYING, "GOD WILL SURELY VISIT YOU, AND YOU SHALL CARRY UP MY BONES FROM HERE"

Joseph died in Egypt, but before he died he made the people of Israel swear that his bones, when God delivered them, would not be left in Egypt.

Notice that Joseph told them, "God will certainly visit you, and when God visits you, do not leave my bones here." This means that the bones have to do with the visitation of God. Joseph relates the visitation of God with his bones. It was very important for Joseph that his bones did not stay in Egypt.

In Exodus 13:19 comes the fulfillment of this promise that the people of Israel made to Joseph.

Exodus 13:19 "AND MOSES TOOK THE BONES OF JOSEPH WITH HIM, FOR HE HAD PLACED THE CHILDREN OF ISRAEL UNDER A SOLEMN OATH, SAYING, "GOD WILL SURELY VISIT YOU, AND YOU SHALL CARRY UP MY BONES FROM HERE WITH YOU"

It was of the utmost importance for the people of Israel that Moses fulfilled the promise that had been made to Joseph.

Hebrews 11:22 "BY FAITH JOSEPH, WHEN HE WAS DYING, MADE MENTION OF THE DEPARTURE OF THE CHILDREN OF ISRAEL, AND GAVE INSTRUCTIONS CONCERNING HIS BONES."

Bones in the Bible are so important that even in the New Testament the bones of Joseph are mentioned. Note that the bones have to do with the departure of the people of Israel from the bondage of Egypt, and the entrance of the people of Israel into the promised land.

That is why there are many Christians today who are under bondage because their bones are captive, their spirit, which is found in the bones, is dead or asleep. That is why the Bible says that we were dead in our crimes and sins, referring to a spiritual death. Your body was not dead because you were still moving, your soul was not dead because you still had thoughts and emotions, therefore what was dead was your spirit that lies within the bones.

The devil knows that if he succeeds in captivating your bones he captivates your spirit as well, and by having your spirit captive he controls your whole being, because your spirit is the one who makes a union with the Holy Spirit.

YOUTH IS IN YOUR BONES

Job 20:11 "HIS BONES ARE FULL OF HIS YOUTHFUL VIGOR, BUT IT WILL LIE DOWN WITH HIM IN THE DUST"

We as humans worry too much about the outward appearance, but, the true youthfulness is inside us, to be more exact, in the bones.

Let's look at it this way. God said that human beings would live 120 years, and the reality is that the majority of people are dying between 60 and 80 years of age. This means that something is happening without us realizing and now we even see it as normal.

When you see that your external appearance begins to deteriorate it is because something in your bones is not right, because in your bones is the spirit of life, and life is in the blood, and blood is produced within your bones. If that blood is contaminated with iniquity or your bones are ill, then they will be producing ill blood and the blood will irrigate throughout your whole body, forming diseases that medical science can not cure.

EMOTIONAL PROBLEMS DAMAGE THE BONES

Psalms 31:9-10 "HAVE MERCY ON ME, O LORD, FOR I AM IN TROUBLE; MY EYE WASTES AWAY WITH GRIEF, YES, MY SOUL AND MY BODY! FOR MY LIFE IS SPENT WITH GRIEF, AND MY YEARS WITH SIGHING; MY STRENGTH FAILS BECAUSE OF MY INIQUITY, AND MY BONES WASTE AWAY"

If you know a person with premature aging, its because the person has lived in depression, sadness, anguish, pain, or other emotional problems. When a person lives this way, what the psalmist is saying is that his bones are being consumed.

Notice that David is saying that iniquity is the cause for his bones to be wasting away. That is to say if someone is facing very strong emotional problems, that person finds himself without strength and without the desire to do anything; it is certain that in his bones there is iniquity. We explained in the previous chapter that iniquity is in your spirit.

BONES LIKE TO BE JOYFUL

Psalms 51:8 "MAKE ME HEAR JOY AND GLADNESS, THAT THE BONES YOU HAVE BROKEN MAY REJOICE"

What David is saying is that his bones are weary because of sadness and suffering. He is now asking God to recreate his bones because he wants to feel joyful and happy. The word recreate begins with the prefix "*RE*", which means to go back to its original state. What David is saying is that if God gives him joy and makes him feel joyful, his bones will return to their original state as they were formed.

That is why it is of the utmost importance that we understand that it is necessary to live always joyful and happy so that we don't feel broken and sick.

A BAD WOMAN IS LIKE THE MOTH

Proverbs 12:4 "AN EXCELLENT WIFE IS THE CROWN OF HER HUSBAND, BUT SHE WHO CAUSES SHAME IS LIKE ROTTENNESS IN HIS BONES"

If you know moths, you will know that they live off of the wood, they begin to eat the wood little by little and if you do not manage to eradicate that plague, it will end up destroying your house.

King Solomon is saying that bad women are like moths, if you do not fix your problems with your wife, it will end up eating your bones. Rotten bones is now commonly known as osteoporosis. A bone sick with osteoporosis will always produce diseased blood and consequently there will be other diseases throughout your body.

So, I recommend that you make peace with your wife and live joyful and happy so that you may be healthy.

THE DEVIL TAKES YOUR BONES CAPTIVE

Psalms 141:7 "OUR BONES ARE SCATTERED AT THE MOUTH OF THE GRAVE, AS WHEN ONE PLOWS AND BREAKS UP THE EARTH."

Grave is referring to an area of hell also known as Sheol. It mentions that our bones are scattered at the entrance of hell. What the devil wants is to keep your bones captive in Sheol.

THE IDOLATRY TAKES BONES CAPTIVE

Ezekiel 6:4-5 "THEN YOUR ALTARS SHALL BE DESOLATE, YOUR INCENSE ALTARS SHALL BE BROKEN, AND I WILL CAST DOWN YOUR SLAIN MEN BEFORE YOUR IDOLS. AND I WILL LAY THE CORPSES OF THE CHILDREN OF ISRAEL BEFORE THEIR IDOLS, AND I WILL SCATTER YOUR BONES ALL AROUND YOUR ALTARS"

These verses are talking about idolatry and witchcraft, and God is saying that He will kill those who practice these things and their bones will be scattered.

All those who in their past or present life are practicing these things, their bones are trapped by the devil in a region of captivity. We must through prophetic acts and declarations take the bones out of that region of captivity.

THE BONES HAVE EARS

Ezekiel 37:4 AGAIN HE SAID TO ME: PROPHESY TO THESE BONES, AND SAY TO THEM, 'O DRY BONES, HEAR THE WORD OF THE LORD!"

God gives a command to the prophet to speak to the bones, to prophesy to them, and to listen to the voice of the Lord. God is saying this to the prophet because He knows that the bones can hear what you speak to them.

TESTIMONY

In our ministry we have experienced this many times. Not only I but also our disciples who speak to the bones of legs and arms which become equal in length when at one point they were uneven. They have spoken to the bones of the neck and spine when the bones are not in their correct position and the bones obeyed and align themselves.

SPIRIT OF LIFE IS IN THE BONES

Ezekiel 37:5 "THUS SAYS THE LORD GOD TO THESE BONES: SURELY I WILL CAUSE BREATH TO ENTER YOU, AND YOU SHALL LIVE"

With this verse we prove once again that God himself is saying that He will put the spirit of life in the bones because it is talking about living.

We have to understand that the subject of bones in the Bible is of the utmost importance. It is a subject like many others that are in secret, as if the revelation of God has not arrived and for that reason we ignore them.
Thanks to God that these are the times when He is revealing all things.

BONES IN WITCHCRAFT

Bones have spiritual power and the witches know this. They use the bones of dead people to do witchcraft or evil to living people. They grind them and make dust of them to work with the bones. This is an abomination before the eyes of God.

NECROMANCY

1 Kings 13:2 "THEN HE CRIED OUT AGAINST THE ALTAR BY THE WORD OF THE LORD, AND SAID, 'O ALTAR, ALTAR!THUS SAYS THE LORD: 'BEHOLD, A CHILD, JOSIAH BY NAME, SHALL BE BORN TO THE HOUSE OF DAVID; AND ON YOU HE SHALL SACRIFICE THE PRIESTS OF THE HIGH PLACES WHO BURN INCENSE ON YOU, AND MEN'S BONES SHALL BE BURNED ON YOU"

In necromancy corpses are used, including their bones to have communication with the dead or try to understand hidden things.

Let's take a look at this verse. The prophet is prophesying to the altar and is telling it that the time will come when a son of the house of David will be born and kill all witches who practiced necromancy on those altars.

FULFILLMENT OF THE PROPHECY

2 Kings 23:16 "AS JOSIAH TURNED, HE SAW THE TOMBS THAT WERE THERE ON THE MOUNTAIN. AND HE SENT AND TOOK THE BONES OUT OF THE TOMBS AND BURNED THEM ON THE ALTAR, AND DEFILED IT ACCORDING TO THE WORD OF THE LORD WHICH THE MAN OF GOD PROCLAIMED, WHO PROCLAIMED THESE WORDS."

In this verse, the prophecy from the previous passage is fulfilled. Note that only the prophets can seize the bones and only when God mandates. If we read all that Josiah did, we are going to realize that he was responsible for overthrowing and destroying all the altars and high places of idolatry in Israel, and he did it by God's command.

THE SPIRIT OF LIFE IS IN THE BONES

2 Kings 13:21 "SO IT WAS, AS THEY WERE BURYING A MAN, THAT SUDDENLY THEY SPIED A BAND OF RAIDERS; AND THEY PUT THE MAN IN THE TOMB OF ELISHA; AND WHEN THE MAN WAS LET DOWN AND TOUCHED THE BONES OF ELISHA, HE REVIVED AND STOOD ON HIS FEET."

So much is the union of the spirit of life in the bones of a son of God, that even the bones of a dead son of God can do miracles. This was the case in the prophet Elisha.

Witches know that when a true child of God dies, they can not work with their bones. And if they do not know, the devil does not let them seize those bones because they are in danger that the spirit of life that is within the bones of a son of God may be transferred to them and their spirit also may be resurrected.

PROPHECY FOR JESUS

Psalms 34:20 "HE GUARDS ALL HIS BONES; NOT ONE OF THEM IS BROKEN."

Is the issue of bones to God so important that He did not allow the bones of His son be touched?

Let's see the fulfillment of this prophecy.
John 19:33 "BUT WHEN THEY CAME TO JESUS AND SAW THAT HE WAS ALREADY DEAD, THEY DID NOT BREAK HIS LEGS."

In this verse we see the fulfillment of Psalm 34:20. God Himself did not allow for the bones of the Son to be touched. The spirit of life is in the bones and it was necessary for Jesus to resurrect on the third day.

CONCLUSION

We have to understand that working with bones is witchcraft and God does not like it for there is a spiritual force in them and it can be transferred.

With all this information about bones I hope you understand that bones in the spiritual realm are very important. The devil takes your bones captive and deposits them in a region of captivity and begins to control you from there.

A person with captive bones is a person with a captive spirit. That is why when you talk and talk to someone about Christ, they really don't want to know anything about Him. It's because their spirit is either dead or asleep, whichever the case may be.

In order to recover the bones out of any region of captivity, all you have to do are prophetic acts as we saw in the previous chapters. You may do so by faith or God may allow you to see where they are buried.

CHAPTER IV

REGIONS OF CAPTIVITY

The Bible speaks of many regions of captivity, which we are going to see in this chapter. In these regions is where the devil has the designs of the souls of your family, churches, cities and even entire countries. It is necessary that the church get to know the regions of captivity and their characteristics to be able to identify in which region the people are captive in and to be more effective in helping them experience freedom in Christ.

If you want to learn more about this subject I recommend a book written by the prophetess Ana Mendez called "Regions of Captivity". This book has been a great blessing to many people around the world.

Let us see some regions of captivity.

LOWEST PIT

Psalms 88:6,8 "YOU HAVE LAID ME IN THE LOWEST PIT, IN DARKNESS, IN THE DEPTHS, YOU HAVE PUT AWAY MY ACQUAINTANCES FROM ME; YOU HAVE MADE ME AN ABOMINATION TO THEM; I AM SHUT UP, AND CANNOT GET OUT"

There are many people who feel that they are locked in a very deep and dark hole. They feel trapped and unable to get out. They feel that their friends have abandoned them. They are locked in a region of captivity, and they are unable to get out by their own strength. They need someone to give them a hand and pull them out of that region in which they find themselves.

THE PRISON

Psalms 142:7 "BRING MY SOUL OUT OF PRISON, THAT I MAY PRAISE YOUR NAME; THE RIGHTEOUS SHALL SURROUND ME, FOR YOU SHALL DEAL BOUNTIFULLY WITH ME"

This verse is not talking about a physical prison, but rather a spiritual prison. He says that his soul is locked up, but a soul is invisible, therefore it cannot be placed in a physical prison. David is saying that he can not praise God because his soul is locked up in a prison. This means that every Christian who can not praise God has a fragment of their soul locked in prison. The soul fragment must be extracted from the region of captivity called prison in order to be set free and be able to praise God.

PIT OF DESPAIR

Psalms 40:2 "HE LIFTED ME OUT OF THE PIT OF DESPAIR, OUT OF THE MUD AND THE MIRE. HE SET MY FEET ON SOLID GROUND AND STEADIED ME AS I WALKED ALONG."

Anyone who has felt or feels despair lies in this region of captivity called the pit of despair. When a person is in depression, distressed, sad, desperate as a result of any difficult situation in life and feels that they cannot get out. They feel like they sink more and more each day. A fragment of their soul is in the region of captivity called the pit of despair.

THE SHEOL

Psalms 49:14 "LIKE SHEEP THEY ARE LAID IN THE GRAVE; DEATH SHALL FEED ON THEM; THE UPRIGHT SHALL HAVE DOMINION OVER THEM IN THE MORNING; AND THEIR BEAUTY SHALL BE CONSUMED IN THE GRAVE, FAR FROM THEIR DWELLING"

Those that are sick are usually found in this region of captivity called the grave or "sheol". When you see a person whose face looks emaciated, or even reflects death, death is shepherding them. If they are not free from that region, then sheol will be their dwelling place.

Psalms 30:2-3 "O LORD MY GOD, I CRIED OUT TO YOU, AND YOU HEALED ME. O LORD, YOU BROUGHT MY SOUL UP FROM THE GRAVE; YOU HAVE KEPT ME ALIVE, THAT I SHOULD NOT GO DOWN TO THE PIT"

David is saying that he was sick and that his soul was in Sheol. Therefore meaning, that the soul of those who are sick are in the region of captivity called Sheol.

That's why there are many sick people that medical science cannot cure. It's not a physical disease, but rather spiritual.

DESTRUCTION

Revelation 9:11 "AND THEY HAD AS KING OVER THEM THE ANGEL OF THE BOTTOMLESS PIT, WHOSE NAME IN HEBREW IS ABADDON, BUT IN GREEK HE HAS THE NAME APOLLYON"

The word abaddon means destruction. In this region you will find people who are always passing through some type of destruction in which their money does not last.
The washing machine, the refrigerator, the blender, the car, the house, someone from the family gets sick or they do themselves, etc. Something is always happening to them. The devil destroys to see them in misery.

You have to extract your soul fragment from that region of captivity through prophetic acts, as we have taught in previous chapters, to be free of what is happening to you.

THE SHADOW OF THE VALLEY OF DEATH

Psalms 107:10-11 "THOSE WHO SAT IN DARKNESS AND IN THE SHADOW OF DEATH, BOUND IN AFFLICTION AND IRONS--- BECAUSE THEY REBELLED AGAINST THE WORDS OF GOD, AND DESPISED THE COUNSEL OF THE MOST HIGH"

These people are imprisoned in darkness and the shadow of death. They feel imprisoned and in distress. The reason they are in that region is because of their rebellion towards God. Every person who rebels against God is going to find himself in these conditions. They have to repent from their disobedience unto God to be free of that captivity.

THE LAND OF FORGETFULNESS

Psalms 88:12"SHALL YOUR WONDERS BE KNOWN IN THE DARK? AND YOUR RIGHTEOUSNESS IN THE LAND OF FORGETFULNESS?"

The people who are not thought about or who are always forgotten, are in the land of the Forgotten, other people even forget these peoples names.
For example the pastor could be praying for all of the members in a line and he skips the person who is in the land of the forgotten, at work they are never promoted or in school they usually do not have friends.

TESTIMONY

One of the pastors who is under my coverage in Mexico told me the following: "When we had the pastors' meeting, they did not take me into account. I wanted to give an opinion and I was not heard, I felt rejected by the other pastors, I spoke to no one. But, when I came to a Supernatural Retreat, I was delivered from regions of captivity. Specifically from the land of forgetfulness and my life changed. When I returned to my city, everyone spoke to me, Many Christians friend requested me on Facebook. Now in the pastors meetings, they listen to me and even ask me for advice. My life has changed and now I preached at another level. "

We could continue to talk about many more regions of captivity. What I want is for you to understand that they exist, and that the devil has fragments of your soul in that region with a design to control your life. But, how does the devil get fragments of your life? Let's look at the next verse to explain it.

Isaiah 7:6 "LET US GO UP AGAINST JUDAH AND TROUBLE IT, AND LET US MAKE A GAP IN ITS WALL FOR OURSELVES, AND SET KING OVER THEM, THE SON OF TABEL"

As I explained in the chapter of designs, this verse is also used in this chapter, Regions of Captivity.

Judah is one of the twelve tribes of Israel and Israel is the people of God. We are also the people of God or the church. Therefore this verse would be saying: "let's go up against the church," or "against you" if we apply it in a personal point of view.

"Let's place fear" This phrase place fear is referring to us or specifically to you. I believe that most people, in some point in life, have been afraid. Therefore, this verse is already fulfilled over you.

"Let's split it up between us." I just clarified that God will never place fear upon you or anyone else. The only one who works with fear is the devil. So, this verse is not God's word but rather the devil's.

After he has already frightened you, he says "fragment the soul to split it among us." That is why when a person is frightened they feel as though their soul has left them or feel a hole inside of them. This is where we hear the phrase: my soul aches or you stole my heart.

After he has frightened you, broken your soul, and divided it. Now, in that hollow place, he places a prince named Tabel. Tabel means good for nothing, what the devil wants is for you to be worthless. That fragment of your soul that the devil robbed from you is taken to a region of captivity and from there he begins to control your life through that design.

Fragments of your soul are not only stolen through fear fragments can also be stolen through those who have practiced witchcraft, idolatry, sects, or people that are sentimentally attached to someone or something.

A LIBERATING GENERATION

Isaiah 42:7 " TO OPEN BLIND EYES, TO BRING OUT PRISONERS FROM THE PRISON, THOSE WHO SIT IN DARKNESS FROM THE PRISON HOUSE"

What the prophet is saying is that God wants a generation of liberators to arise. To rescue captives out of the regions of captivity. That is why he says that we should liberate prisoners out of prison houses or jail cells. To those who live in darkness.

Isaiah 51:14 "THE CAPTIVE EXILE HASTENS, THAT HE MAY BE LOOSED, THAT HE SHOULD NOT DIE IN THE PIT, AND THAT HIS BREAD SHOULD NOT FAIL."

This prophecy is referring to Jesus coming to liberate the captives.

The fulfillment of the prophecy is in *Luke 4:18*:
"THE SPIRIT OF THE LORD IS UPON ME, BECAUSE HE HAS ANOINTED ME TO PREACH THE GOSPEL TO THE POOR; HE HAS SENT ME TO HEAL THE BROKENHEARTED, TO PROCLAIM LIBERTY TO THE CAPTIVES AND RECOVER OF SIGHT TO THE BLIND, TO SET LIBERTY TO THOSE WHO ARE OPPRESSED;"

Jesus came to the earth, and left us a commandment which most people are not fulfilling. We are to be doing the same thing that He did when He was here on earth.

Isaiah 49:24-25 "SHALL THE PREY BE TAKEN FROM THE MIGHTY, OR THE RIGHTEOUS BE DELIVERED? BUT THUS SAYS THE LORD: EVEN THE CAPTIVES OF THE MIGHTY SHALL BE TAKEN AWAY, AND THE PREY OF THE TERRIBLE BE DELIVERED; FOR I WILL CONTEND WITH HIM WHO CONTENDS WITH YOU, AND I WILL SAVE YOUR CHILDREN."

Isaiah 58:6 "IS THIS NOT THE FAST THAT I HAVE CHOSEN: TO LOOSE THE BONDS OF WICKEDNESS, TO UNDO THE HEAVY BURDENS, TO LET THE OPPRESSED GO FREE, AND THAT YOU BREAK EVERY YOKE?"

What God wants is for you and I to be the ones to set the captives free. For years we have been taught in the temples theology and religion which does not save anyone. The proof is that those same pastors are in captivity in some areas of their life. Enough of so much religion that has done so much damage to humanity. Let us be that generation that God is raising in the last days to free the captives.

Apostle Moises Ramirez

CHAPTER V

COVENANT OF SALT

In this chapter we will talk about the salt covenant. Is it not for our times? If its current, did somebody take it from us and we didn't even notice? We will see what the Bible tells us about it.

Matthew 5:13 "YOU ARE THE SALT OF THE EARTH; BUT IF THE SALT LOOSES ITS FLAVOR, HOW SHALL IT BE SEASONED? IT IS THEN GOOD FOR NOTHING BUT TO BE THROWN OUT AND TRAMPLED UNDERFOOT OF MAN"

In order to understand this verse, we need to know the properties and functions of the salt, so we can fulfill this verse.
It says that salt can lose its flavor and be trampled by men. In this chapter we will be learning about the "Salt Covenant".

FUNCTIONS OF THE SALT

The salt is good for:
1- Flavor
2- Conservation
3- Reduce inflammation
4- Disinfect
5- Clean
6- To Scar
7- Block bleeding

All these functions and maybe even more are done with salt and Jesus said that we are the salt of the earth.

FLAVOR

The children of God are responsible for giving flavor to this world. Do you realize what this world would be like without the children of God? It would be full of confusion, chaos and evil. Is this not the case in the world in which we live in? Yes, it is. Then it means that the salt has lost its flavor and has become insipid where men are trampling it.

The truth is that the church has become insipid for a long time. We need to understand that the hope for this world is Jesus Christ through his church. It is time that we become a granite of salt to give flavor to this world.

CONSERVES

Another function of salt is to conserve. I remember when I was a teenage boy, at my parent's ranch, they would cover the meat with salt and hang it outside to dry with the sun. The meat did not spoil nor the flies bother it.

If the Bible says that we are salt and salt conserves, the question is: What are we conserving? On the contrary, we are destroying more and more the earth and destroying ourselves. That is why the Bible says that the earth is waiting for the manifestation of the children of God. It is time that the children of God begin to rise up and begin to be salt to conserve this land, families and ourselves.

DISINFECT, REDUCE INFLAMMATION, TO SCAR AND STOP HEMORRHAGES

At the ranch, my father would castrate a male animal, whether it be a pig, a goat, etc... Once he was finished, he would place salt around the wound so that it would not become infected or inflamed. At the same time heal and stop the bleeding of the animal.

We are the salt of the earth, and we are also earth because we were formed from the dust of the earth.
There are many "earths" called humans that are suffering from so many wounds that they are dragging from their past with no salt to cover them because the salt has become insipid and useless. That's how Christians are today, without being the salt we do not heal anyone's wounds, we do not help scar their wounds and that's why they're bleeding from the inside.

It is time to become the salt to disinfect and stop the inflammation of humanity that is suffering and bleeding.

Let's look at some texts in the Bible that talk about salt.

Genesis 19:26 "BUT HIS WIFE LOOKED BACK BEHIND HIM, AND SHE BECAME A PILLAR OF SALT."

This is the first verse in the Bible that speaks of salt, referring to the destruction of Sodom and Gomorrah. When Lot and his family left the city to be free of destruction, Lot's wife looked back and she became a statue of salt.
Everything that has to do with Sodom and Gomorrah also involves salt. You will understand as we go forward and see more Biblical texts.

Lot's wife looked back. This means that anyone who turns back in their spiritual life has to do with a curse of salt.

THE SALT AND OFFERINGS

Mark 9:49 " FOR EVERYONE WILL BE SEASONED WITH FIRE, AND EVERY SACRIFICE WILL BE SEASONED WITH SALT"

Every sacrifice has to have salt. A sacrifice was an offering that God had commanded to be offered unto Him.

Leviticus 2:13 "AND EVERY OFFERING OF YOUR GRAIN OFFERING YOU SHALL SEASON WITH SALT; YOU SHALL NOT ALLOW THE SALT COVENANT OF YOUR GOD TO BE LACKING FROM YOUR GRAIN OFFERING. WITH ALL YOUR OFFERINGS YOU SHALL OFFER SALT"

God gave them commandment of how offerings should be offered unto Him. God told them, "All the offerings shall have salt " and clarifies to them, "for it is a covenant."

Ezekiel 43:23-24 "WHEN YOU HAVE FINISHED CLEANSING IT, YOU SHALL OFFER A YOUNG BULL WITHOUT BLEMISH, AND A RAM FROM THE FLOCK WITHOUT BLEMISH. WHEN YOU OFFER BEFORE THE LORD, THE PRIEST SHALL THROW SALT ON THEM, AND THEY WILL OFFER THEM UP AS A BURNT OFFERING TO THE LORD"

God told his people, "When you have finished the atonement for your sin, you are going to bring me an offering of an animal without defect. You will bring it to the temple and the priests will place salt upon the offering. "

Why would God tell his people that they should place salt upon it? Because salt, as in the natural, has several functions also in the spiritual.

THE SALT IN THE SPIRITUAL SPHERE

Salt in the spiritual sphere serves to:
1- To curse
2- To Bless

That's why witches and other people working in the spiritual realm of darkness use salt.

With salt they curse marriages, businesses, families, cities, etc... They can cause diseases of all kinds, cause business failure, bind couples and even kill people.

Where did they learn these things and how to use the salt? Who taught them? The devil knows the Bible more than many of us. He took everything from the bible but did the opposite. He took a Biblical truth and twisted it. A truth that belongs to the people of God and not to the children of the devil. The Bible says that the children of darkness are more astute than the children of light.

But the salt also serves to bless. All the curses that the witches provoke with the salt, with the same salt, you can undo all work of the devil upon your life and your family. Returning to the passage of Ezekiel 43:24. God told his people that they should put salt to all the offerings because the salt also cleanses spiritually. Every offering should be without defect and without spiritual contamination.

THE SALT IN TODAY'S OFFERINGS

If we continue to practice the commandment of the offerings today, how are you offering your offerings unto God? Is the money you give to God polluted? Do you know what the money in your wallet was used for? Is your gift that you are giving to God dirty? Is that why you do not see any results in your offerings and tithes? What if, with the currency you offer to God, drugs were purchased, used to pay for a prostitute, used to have someone murdered and blood was shed. Maybe it was used to consult a witch doctor or purchased stolen items, etc... And now you come to the temple and bring a polluted offering to God. Do you believe that God is going to receive a dirty, contaminated, and sinful offering? I personally believe that God is not going to receive an offering in these conditions. That is why He gave command to his people, that "all", "all" offerings must carry salt. With salt, the offerings, are spiritually cleansed of all spiritual contamination.

In addition, you take home spirits of prostitution, drug addiction, diseases, witchcraft, death, and many more demons with money that has been spiritually contaminated.

THE SALT COVENANT IS PERPETUAL

Numbers 18:19 "ALL THE HEAVE OFFERINGS OF THE HOLY THINGS, WHICH THE CHILDREN OF ISRAEL OFFER TO THE LORD, I HAVE GIVEN TO YOU AND YOUR SONS AND DAUGHTERS WITH YOU AS AN ORDINANCE FOREVER; IT IS A COVENANT OF SALT FOREVER BEFORE THE LORD WITH YOU AND YOUR DESCENDANTS WITH YOU."

Perpetual = Everlasting or has no end.

If the covenant of salt is everlasting and God commanded His children to put salt on the offerings, what has happened to the salt in the offerings of today? Is it also a salt covenant for us? If He says that it is for His children and their offspring, are we children of God?

Church, God is a God of covenants. In the course of the history of humanity God has made covenants with His children. Every covenant of God with His children brings blessings and protection. The devil knows this and has stolen the truth. Over the years he has robbed us from the salt covenant like many other Biblical truths.

Because no one taught us and we see that the devil's children use salt, we think it's witchcraft. But it was God who created salt and not the devil. God gave it to His people as a perpetual covenant of salt.

How is it possible that the children of the devil are using the salt to curse humanity? And the people of God stay calm and doing nothing?

Its time for the church to realize this truth and recover what belongs to it, the salt covenant.

Grab your money, wallet, or purse and clean it with salt. Cancel any spiritual contamination upon your money before offering it to God and you will soon see results.

Deuteronomy 29:23 "THE WHOLE LAND IS BRIMSTONE, SALT, AND BURNING; IT IS NOT SOWN, NOR DOES IT BEAR, NOR DOES ANY GRASS GROW THERE, LIKE THE OVERTHROW OF SODOM AND GOMORRAH, ADMAH, AND ZEBOIM, WHICH THE LORD OVERTHREW IN HIS ANGER AND HIS WRATH."

This land is cursed by God with sulfur and salt as it did with Sodom and Gomorrah. These cities were destroyed with salt.

Here the salt is used by God himself to curse those cities that were full of witchcraft and sexual perversion. Everything that has to do with witchcraft and sexual perversion is canceled with salt.

There are many Bible scriptures that talk about salt. I will mention a few and you may read them, take your time.

1 - Zephaniah 2:9	Moab & Ammon= Children of incest.
2 - Joshua 15:62	NIBSHAN = Fertile soil.
3 - 2 Samuel 8:13	Valley of salt.
4 - 2 Kings 14:7a	Valley of salt.
5 - 2 Chronicles 25:11	Valley of salt.
6 - Psalms 60	David defeated his enemies in the valley of salt.
7 - Judges 9:45	Spread salt throughout the city for his enemies no longer to rise.
8 - Ezra 6:9-10	Offerings of wine, salt, and oil.
9 - Ezekiel 47:1-11	A river is healed by sea salt and the swamps are not.

LAND AND WATERS ARE HEALED WITH SALT

2 Kings 2:19-21 "THEN THE MEN OF THE CITY SAID TO ELISHA, PLEASE NOTICE, THE SITUATION OF THIS CITY IS PLEASANT, AS MY LORD SEES; BUT THE WATER IS BAD, AND THE GROUND BARREN. AND HE SAID, BRING ME A NEW BOWL, AND PUT SALT IN IT. SO THEY BROUGHT IT TO HIM. THEN HE WENT OUT TO THE SOURCE OF WATER, AND CAST IN THE SALT THERE, AND SAID, THUS SAYS THE LORD: I HAVE HEALED THIS WATER; FROM IT THERE SHALL BE NO MORE DEATH OR BARRENNESS"

The land and waters were cursed and as a result the land was barren and the waters produced disease and death. The prophet healed them with salt and everything returned to normal.

61

The earth, because of the sin of Adam, God cursed it. The more sin humanity commits, the more earth is cursed. In the beginning, the earth produced the riches that Adam needed to live.

Today, the earth and humanity are in enmity. Therefore earth is no longer producing as it should produce. The earth is waiting for the manifestation of the children of God.

Heal the piece of land that belongs to you. Ask for forgiveness, clean the land of all blood spilled on it, become a friend of the land and you will see what it does for you. The earth is vomiting its inhabitants, unable to get along. The earth is crying, moaning, and shouting, Where are the children of God? If we could hear the voice of earth, it would tell us: "Because of you I am suffering, you are destroying me, stop sinning, do not shed more blood on me, and ask me for forgiveness. Then I will give you what you need."

SALT ON THE NEWLY BORN BABIES

Ezekiel 16:4-6 "AS FOR YOUR NATIVITY, ON THE DAY YOU WERE BORN YOUR NAVEL CORD WAS NOT CUT, NOR WERE YOU WASHED IN WATER TO CLEANSE YOU; YOU WERE NOT RUBBED WITH SALT NOR WRAPPED IN SWADDLING CLOTHS. NO EYE PITIED YOU, TO DO ANY OF THESE THINGS FOR YOU, TO HAVE COMPASSION ON YOU; BUT YOU WERE THROWN OUT INTO THE OPEN FIELD, WHEN YOU YOURSELF WERE LOATHED ON THE DAY YOU WERE BORN. AND WHEN I PASSED BY YOU AND SAW YOU STRUGGLING IN YOUR OWN BLOOD, I SAID TO YOU IN YOUR BLOOD, LIVE! YES, I SAID TO YOU IN YOUR BLOOD, LIVE!"

Look at what God is saying. He is comparing Jerusalem to the birth of a baby. He mentions that when a baby is born the umbilical cord is cut, the baby is bathed in water, salt rubbed on the baby, and wrapped in cloths.

All this is still being done today to a baby when it is born, except the rubbing with salt. Once again the devil has stolen the salt covenant.

A baby is born into a spiritual war and that is why you have to rub the baby with salt to clean the baby of all generational curses and the curses that are being thrown at the baby unconsciously.

We say phrases such as "he looks a lot like his dad" and his dad is an adulterer or a drug addict, etc... Without knowing, many relatives are releasing curses upon the newborn baby.

We need to restore the salt covenant that the devil took from us.

PRESENT YOUR BODY AS A SACRIFICE

Romans 12:1 "I BESEECH YOU THEREFORE, BRETHREN, BY THE MERCIES OF GOD, THAT YOU PRESENT YOUR BODIES A LIVING SACRIFICE, HOLY, ACCEPTABLE TO GOD, WHICH YOUR REASONABLE SERVICE."

The Apostle Paul says that we should present our bodies in sacrifice. And every sacrifice must have salt. If you want to present yourself before God as a living sacrifice and be accepted, then clean the sacrifice with salt, because every sacrifice must have salt.

WE ARE THE SALT OF THE EARTH

Matthew 5:13 "YOU ARE THE SALT OF THE EARTH; BUT IF THE SALT LOSES ITS FLAVOR, HOW SHALL IT BE SEASONED? IT IS THEN GOOD FOR NOTHING BUT TO BE THROWN OUT AND TRAMPLED UNDERFOOT OF MEN."

We conclude this chapter with the same passage that we started with. Now you understand more what Jesus meant when He said that we are the salt of the earth.

If a child of God is not asserting the functions of the salt, it has become tasteless and surely they are being trampled upon.

HOW TO KNOW IF I AM SALT?

When you arrive to a place and change the atmosphere. At work or school your co-workers or friends respect you and say: "shut up, do not say bad words because the brother has arrived", or hide the cigar, or stop drinking, etc... When this happens, you are salt. When you arrive at an empty store or restaurant and then its filled with customers. You, the salt, has cleansed the environment and transformed the atmosphere.

But when no one respects you, your friends are still drinking, smoking, or saying bad words in front of you, you have lost the flavor. You have became insipid salt and the children of men are trampling you.

It is time for you to put into practice all the knowledge of this teaching upon your life, your family, your land, and your city. Let us heal the land from the evil that is happening in the world. We are responsible for transforming the environment around us.

Apostle Moises Ramirez

CHAPTER VI

HOLY SUPPER

The book of Acts is a mirror for the church of our times. if we can fully reflect on that mirror, we are going to realize that the church of our times does not resemble the church of the book of Acts.

Let's look at just one feature of the primitive church

Acts 2:42-47 "AND THEY CONTINUED STEADFASTLY IN THE APOSTLES' DOCTRINE AND FELLOWSHIP, IN THE BREAKING OF BREAD, AND IN PRAYERS. THEN FEAR CAME UPON EVERY SOUL, AND MANY WONDERS AND SIGNS WERE DONE THROUGH THE APOSTLES. NOW ALL WHO BELIEVED WERE TOGETHER, AND HAD ALL THINGS IN COMMON, AND SOLD THEIR POSSESSIONS AND GOODS, AND DIVIDED THEM AMONG ALL, AS ANYONE HAD NEED. SO CONTINUING DAILY WITH ONE ACCORD I THE TEMPLE, AND BREAKING BREAD FROM HOUSE TO HOUSE, THEY ATE THEIR FOOD WITH GLADNESS AND SIMPLICITY OF HEART, PRAISING GOD AND HAVING FAVOR WITH ALL THE PEOPLE. AND THE LORD ADDED TO THE CHURCH DAILY THOSE WHO WERE BEING SAVED."

Let's take a look at these verses. The early church lived in signs and wonders every day and had favor of all the people. The church of today does not have the people's favor. Has no signs and wonders. Because of Christian's testimony, people do not want to be part of the church. The outcome of signs and wonders was that God added to the church, those who were open to salvation. Notice that it was the Lord who added them, not you, not the pastor, the people alone wanted to be part of that group of believers.

The New Testament church had a good reputation within the village. Today, Christians have ruined the reputation within their own home. It is sad to see many who claim to be Christians ruin the testimony of those who do things as God commands.

In Acts 2:42 we see four things that the primitive church did. If we succeeded in understanding and do these four things, we will be conducting ourselves as God wants His church to walk.

Acts 2:42 "AND THEY CONTINUED STEADFASTLY IN THE APOSTLES' DOCTRINE AND FELLOWSHIP, IN THE BREAKING OF BREAD, AND IN PRAYERS."

1- DOCTRINE OF THE APOSTLES: Today, many do not believe in the apostles.
2-FELLOWSHIP WITH ONE ANOTHER: The primitive church had all things in common and were united. Today even the pastors themselves are fighting with each other.

3-THE LORD'S SUPPER: They participated in the holy supper of the Lord in their homes. Today, many churches no longer practice the Lord's Supper.

4- PRAYER: Prayer is key for a church to stand firm. The overall average for Christians is 5 to 10 minutes of prayer a day. And that's the way we want to be a victorious church?

These four things that the primitive church practiced transformed the world. If we succeed in understanding and practice what they did, we will have the church that Christ established. But, let's just talk about one of them...

THE LORD'S SUPPER

To partake of the Lord's supper is to institute the Melchizedek Priesthood.

Genesis 14:18-20 "THEN MELCHIZEDEK KING OF SALEM BROUGHT OUT BREAD AND WINE; HE WAS THE PRIEST OF GOD MOST HIGH. AND HE BLESSED HIM AND SAID: BLESSED BE ABRAM OF GOD MOST HIGH, POSSESSOR OF HEAVEN AND EARTH; AND BLESSED BE GOD MOST HIGH, WHO HAS DELIVERED YOUR ENEMIES INTO YOUR HAND. AND GAVE HIM A TITHE OF ALL."

What is happening here is a foreshadowing of what would happen later. This scripture is a covenant of God to Abram. God gives him the body and blood of his son Jesus and Abram gives him the tithes of everything.

This is fulfilled when Jesus surrendered His life on the cross and we accept him as our savior and give Him our tithes. If you want to live under the covering of this covenant, be faithful to God with your tithes.

TRADITION OR REVELATION

Matthew 26:26-28 "AND AS THEY WERE EATING, JESUS TOOK BREAD, BLESSED AND BROKE IT, AND GAVE IT TO THE DISCIPLES AND SAID, TAKE, EAT; THIS IS MY BODY. THEN HE TOOK THE CUP, AND GAVE THANKS, AND GAVE IT TO THEM, SAYING, DRINK FROM IT, ALL OF YOU. FOR THIS IS MY BLOOD OF THE NEW COVENANT, WHICH IS SHED FOR THE REMISSION OF SINS."

Today there are many churches that are no longer celebrating the Lord's Supper. Some do so by tradition, ignoring the true revelation of what this implies.

These are direct words the Lord Jesus said. The bread is His body, not that the bread symbolizes His body. I will explain this in more detail later. And the second thing that He tells us, is for all to participate. He made no exceptions of people, like many do today. Remember that Peter who hours later would deny Him and Judas who would betray Him, were there. Allowing us to understand that the covenant of Lord's Supper is reaffirming what Melchizedek did.

COMMUNION IS THE LORD'S SUPPER

1 Corinthians 10:16-17 "THE CUP OF BLESSING WHICH WE BLESS, IS IT NOT THE COMMUNION OF THE BLOOD OF CHRIST? THE BREAD WHICH WE BREAK, IS IT NOT THE COMMUNION OF THE BODY OF CHRIST? FOR WE, THOUGH MANY, ARE ONE BREAD AND ONE BODY; FOR WE ALL PARTAKE OF THAT ONE BREAD."

In this verse, the apostle Paul is calling the Lord's Supper: communion.

COMMUNION = COINONIA = Fellowship, friendship, common union, sharing something with someone.

God demonstrated coinonia with mankind by sharing His son with us. The body of Christ should always unite us. Not religion, doctrine of men, or organizations. Look at all the churches around us divided by the lack of revelation of the Lord's Supper.

Notice that the apostle Paul also says the same thing that Jesus mentioned in the book of Matthew: "For we all partake of that same bread",reaffirming "all" partake of the body of Christ, without the exception of persons.

The apostle Paul says in 1 Corinthians 11:23 that what he taught them, he received it directly from the Lord.

PAUL RECEIVES IT WITH REVELATION

1 Corinthians 11:23-26 "FOR I RECEIVED FROM THE LORD THAT WHICH I ALSO DELIVERED TO YOU: THAT THE LORD JESUS ON THE DAY HE WAS BETRAYED TOOK BREAD; AND WHEN HE HAD GIVEN THANKS, HE BROKE IT AND SAID, TAKE,

EAT; THIS IS MY BODY WHICH IS BROKEN FOR YOU; DO THIS IN REMEMBRANCE OF ME. IN THE SAME MANNER HE ALSO TOOK THE CUP AFTER SUPPER, SAYING, THIS CUP IS THE NEW COVENANT IN MY BLOOD. THIS DO, AS OFTEN AS YOU DRINK

IT, IN REMEMBRANCE OF ME. FOR AS OFTEN AS YOU EAT THIS BREAD AND DRINK THIS CUP, YOU PROCLAIM THE LORD'S DEATH TILL HE COMES."

Notice that they are the same words that Jesus spoke in Mathew referring to the fact that bread is the body and the wine is the blood of Christ.

In verse 24 and 25 it says that when you eat His body and drink His blood, we do so in "memory of Him"

IN MEMORY OF ME

The phrase in memory of me has a great meaning. He is saying that we must return to the time and place where Jesus was crucified.

"In memory of me" is more than simply remembering what they did to Jesus. It is to live and feel what Jesus felt. In other words, feel the lashes as Jesus felt them, when you partake of the Lord's supper "do it in remembrance of me says the Lord Jesus." That is, feel what he felt, feel the crown of thorns on your forehead, feel the nails in your hands, feel the nails on your feet, feel the spear on your side, feel the blood running all over your body. Do it in memory of him, do not partake of the Lord's supper just by tradition but by revelation.

In verse 26 it says, "The Lord's death you announce until He comes." The apostle Paul is saying that every time we partake of the Lord's Supper we announce the death of Jesus. The question is, to whom do you announce death Of the Lord Jesus? It is announced to the physical and the spiritual world.

THE NATURAL OR PHYSICAL WORLD

The physical world is humanity. If you participate in the Lord's supper as it should be, your life will change. People will notice and will want to be like you. Was this happening in the primitive church?

SPIRITUAL WORLD

When we partake of the Lord's supper with revelation, we are announcing to the devil and his demons what Jesus did to them on the cross of Calvary. He knocked them down, defeated them, disarmed them, destroyed them and publicly displayed them.

The devil is angered when he is reminded of his defeat. The devil did not expect for Jesus to resurrect on the third day. When should you announce the death of the Lord Jesus? Paul says, "Until he comes", and I say, "Every day until he comes."

If we partake of the Lord's supper with these revelations. The meaning of "in memory of me" is to live what he lived and feel what he felt. "The death of the Lord you announce" is to announce to mankind with your testimony and to remind the devil and his demons of their defeat. Finally "All the times you eat" every day the devil is defeated.

RESTORING THE LORD'S SUPPER

John 6:27-58 " DO NOT LABOR FOR THE FOOD WHICH PERISHES, BUT FOR THE FOOD WHICH ENDURES TO EVERLASTING LIFE, WHICH THE SON OF MAN WILL GIVE YOU, BECAUSE GOD THE FATHER HAS SET HIS SEAL ON HIM. "

We are going to be seeing all these verses one by one and explain them so that we can understand clearly the revelation of the Lord's Supper.

God the Father entrusts His son in giving the spiritual food for eternal life. Let's continue talking about spiritual food.

Verse 28 "THEN THEY SAID TO HIM, WHAT SHALL WE DO, THAT WE MAY WORK THE WORKS OF GOD?"

The people who followed Jesus asked Him a question, which is in verse 28. They wanted to do the work of God. If you also want to do God's work, let's see what Jesus' responded.

Verse 29 " JESUS ANSWERED AND SAID TO THEM, THIS IS THE WORK OF GOD, THAT YOU BELIEVE IN HIM WHO HE SENT."

From verses 29 through 58 Jesus answers their question. The first thing He tells them is to believe in Him.

Although it seems a lie, the evangelical churches are full of unbelievers. They only believe what has been taught to them. Aside from that, they do not believe. Some do not believe in the apostles. Some believe more in the devil than God Himself. They believe the devil can do miracles and God is unable to. That's why nothing happens in the churches today. The Bible says, "these signs shall follow them that believe." Then why is nothing happening? Why are we not believing as we should? I hope you believe in its totality and especially in this revelation that you are going to learn today.

Verse 30 "THEREFORE THEY SAID TO HIM, WHAT SIGN WILL YOU PERFORM THEN, THAT WE MIGHT SEE IT AND BELIEVE YOU? WHAT WORK WILL YOU DO?"

People keep asking Him the same thing, because they wanted to know the secret of how He did it, for them to do it too.

JESUS CONTINUES TO ANSWER THE QUESTION

Verses 31-34 "OUR FATHERS ATE MANNA IN THE DESSERT; AS IT IS WRITTEN, HE GAVE THEM BREAD FROM HEAVEN TO EAT. THEN JESUS SAID TO THEM, MOST ASSUREDLY, I SAY TO YOU, MOSES DID NOT GIVE YOU BREAD FROM HEAVEN, BUT MY FATHER GIVES YOU THE TRUE BREAD FROM HEAVEN. FOR THE BREAD OF GOD IS HEWHO COMES DOWN FROM HEAVEN AND GIVES LIFE TO THE WORLD. THEN THEY SAIDTO HIM, LORD, GIVE US THIS BREAD ALWAYS."

Notice the question they asked, and the answer that Jesus gave. Apparently the answer has nothing to do with the question. They want to do the work of God and He answers them about bread, but a bread that gives eternal life.

Verse 35 "AND JESUS SAID TO THEM, I AM THE BREAD OF LIFE. HE WHO COMES TO ME SHALL NEVER HUNGER, AND HE WHO BELIEVES IN ME SHALL NEVER THIRST"

See how Jesus is gradually introducing Himself. Jesus reminds them again that they must believe in Him. Jesus puts two conditions: to come and believe in Him. This is the problem that exists with Christians today. Many say that they believe in Him but do not come Him. Others come but halfway believe.

Verse 36 "BUT I SAID TO YOU THAT YOU HAVE SEEN ME AND YET DO NOT BELIEVE."

Jesus is stressing their disbelief; Those who saw Him did not believe in Him. Now, imagine us who who have not seen Him. They saw everything that Jesus did and still did not believe. I believe that there is more unbelief today than in those times.

Verses 41-42 "THE JEWS THEN COMPLAINED ABOUT HIM, BECAUSE HE SAID, I AM THE BREAD WHICH CAME DOWN FROM HEAVEN. AND THEY SAID, IS NOT THIS JESUS, THE SON OF JOSEPH, WHOSE FATHER AND MOTHER WE KNOW? HOW IS IT THEN HE SAYS, I HAVE COME DOWN FROM HEAVEN?"

People did not believe when He told them that He was the bread that came down from heaven. They began to murmur and I hope you do not start to murmur about what you're going to learn.

Verse 50 "THIS IS THE BREAD WHICH COMES DOWN FROM HEAVEN, THAT ONE MAY EAT OF IT AND NOT DIE."

Jesus repeats to them that He is the bread, and all those who eat of Him are not going to die. He is referring to a spiritual life. We do not die, but sleep.

Verse 51 "I AM THE LIVING BREAD WICH CAME DOWN FROM HEAVEN. IF ANYONE EATS OF THIS BREAD, HE WILL LIVE FOREVER; AND THE BREAD THAT I SHALL GIVE IS MY FLESH, WHICH I SHALL GIVE FOR THE LIFE OF THE WORLD."

Jesus continues to emphasize that He is the bread. But now, He makes a transition and tells them: the bread is My flesh. This is important, notice that He is not telling them that the bread *symbolizes* His flesh, but clarifying that the bread *is* His flesh. That's why He was emphasizing their disbelief first. If He says that bread is His flesh, then I believe it period.

Verses 52-53 "THE JEWS THEREFORE QUARRELED AMONG THEMSELVES, SAYING, HOW CAN THIS MAN GIVE US HIS FLESH TO EAT? THEN JESUS SAID TO THEM, MOST ASSUREDLY, I SAY TO YOU, UNLESS YOU EAT THE FLESH OF THE SON OF MAN AND DRINK HIS BLOOD, YOU HAVE NO LIFE IN YOU."

The Jews did not understand and that's why they were arguing. I hope you do not argue and understand this revelation. Jesus tells them to eat of His flesh and to drink of His blood. This seems like He was talking about cannibalism and vampires, that is why they could not understand Him. Obviously He was referring to something spiritual. Jesus tells them to eat of His flesh and drink His blood so that we may have life.

That's why there are many Christians who have no life. Many are sick and dying for not taking the Lord's supper with revelation.

Verses 54-58 "WHOEVER EATS MY FLESH AND DRINKS MY BLOOD HAS ETERNAL LIFE, AND I WILL RAISE HIM UP AT THE LAST DAY. FOR MY FLESH IS FOOD INDEED, AND MY BLOOD IS DRINK INDEED. HE WHO EATS MY FLESH AND DRINKS MY BLOOD ABIDES IN ME, AND I IN HIM. AS THE LIVING FATHER HAS SENT ME, AND I LIVE BECAUSE OF THE FATHER, SO HE WHO FEEDS ON ME WILL LIVE BECAUSE OF ME. THIS IS THE BREAD WHICH CAME DOWN FROM HEAVEN—NOT AS YOUR FATHERS ATE THE MANNA, AND ARE DEAD. HE WHO EATS THIS BREAD WILL LIVE FOREVER."

Here, Jesus says something very important: that He who eats of His flesh and drinks His blood abides in Him and He with us. This is a problem with Christians today. Many do not know how to stay in Him, and if we do not partake of the Lord's Supper, He does not remain in us.

The revelation of all this, is that when you partake of the communion or the Lord's supper your physical body receives bread, but your spirit receives His flesh. Your physical body receives the wine, but your spirit receives His blood. All these revelations that you are learning, will change your life.

THE DOCTRINE OF TRANSUBSTANTIATION

This doctrine speaks that the bread is the flesh and the wine is the blood of the Lord Jesus Christ. Is this not the same thing that Jesus said in John 6: 27-58 that the bread is His flesh and the wine is His blood and that he must eat His flesh and drink His blood?

This doctrine is saying the same exact thing. But just because this doctrine is taken from the Catholic Church we declare it wrong. We cannot inclose ourselves, no matter who brings it forth. What does matter, is what Jesus said in these passages.

THE DOCTRINE OF CONSUBSTANTIATION

The difference between one and the other is: *"TRAN"* and *"CON"* and what this doctrine means is: "change of substance".

In other words, this doctrine says that the bread symbolizes the flesh of Jesus and the wine symbolizes the blood of Jesus.

But we have already read several passages where Jesus and the apostles speak about the Lord's supper. They never mentioned that the bread and the wine symbolize anything. if we use the word **SYMBOLIZE**, that changes the revelation of the Lord's supper.

The doctrine of consubstantiation was born with the reform of Martin Luther. All evangelical christians were born of the Protestants and we continue to drag this doctrine. But at the end of all, the evangelical christians came from the protestants, and the Protestants from the Catholic Church. In other words, they all came from the Catholic Church. That is why Revelation 17: 5 says "... the mother of all harlots ..."

CONCLUSION

I hope that with this revelation of the Lord's Supper we begin to practice the communion of Christ properly. Every time you want to announce what Jesus did on the cross, do it in His memory, feeling and suffering the same thing that He felt and suffered. For this is the new covenant of God to you. Just as He did with Abram and Abram gave the tithes of everything. The covenant gives you covering and pours blessings upon your life.

I bless you in the name of Jesus Christ.

Apostle Moises Ramirez

CHAPTER VII

ACTIVATE YOUR ANGEL

Angels have existed since before the creation of planet earth. If we read the Bible, we will realize that from Genesis to Revelation it talks about angels.

Angels in the Bible is something very normal. We see how God commanded angels to give messages to men, to protect them, to apply judgment, and to bless someone. When we speak about angels in the Bible it is because they have something to do with men.

Today, the theme of angels is not very common in the Christian church. There are even pastors who do not believe in the existence of angels. In this chapter called "Activate Your Angel" we are going to learn many things about angels that will be of great help to your life.

SERVING ANGELS

Hebrews 1:14 "ARE THEY NOT ALL MINISTERING SPIRITS SENT FORTH TO MINISTER FOR THOSE WHO WILL INHERIT SALVATION?"

In this verse we realize that it is speaking of servant angels, but, he clarifies, that they will serve and care for those who inherit salvation.
I do not know you, but I am an heir of salvation, therefore the angels are my servants and also take care of me.

ANGEL = Messenger
ANGEL = Spiritual beings below men.

JESUS SPOKE OF THEIR EXISTENCE

Matthew 18:10 "TAKE HEED THAT YOU DO NOT DESPISE ONE OF THESE LITTLE ONES, FOR I SAY TO YOU THAT IN HEAVEN THEIR ANGELS ALWAYS SEE THE FACE OF MY FATHER WHO IS IN HEAVEN."

Jesus is talking about the children, that we must be very careful not to despise one of them. Then he says: "their" angels are in the presence of the Father. Giving an understanding that children have angels who care and serve them. In Matthew 26:53 Jesus also spoke of the existence of angels. With these two texts we can accept the existence of angels.

MAN IS GREATER THAN ANGELS

Psalms 8:4-5 " WHAT IS MAN THAT YOU ARE MINDFUL OF HIM, AND THE SON OF MAN THAT YOU VISIT HIM? FOR YOU HAVE MADE HIM A LITTLE LOWER THAN THE ANGELS, AND YOU HAVE CROWNED HIM WITH GLORY AND HONOR. "

In general, this text has done a lot of damage to Christianity because of its poor translation. If you read verse 5 in the NLT translation you are going to realize that the word "*angels*" was translated to "*God*". The original word that is used is "Elohim", which means God.

Then the correct translation is: "You made him a little less than God" If we were to accept that we are less than angels, then we would be saying that the devil, who is a fallen angel, would be greater than us. If he's greater than us, why did God command us to fight him?

But if I take into account the true meaning of this text, then I see things from another point of view. The devil is less than me and therefore has to submit to me. In other words, the devil is a servant of mine, hence the phrase: *"the devil does what I say."*

There are churches that ignore the true meaning of this text and are afraid of the devil. I remember one occasion in a church mentioning something about the devil and the pastor told me, "shut up, do not mention the devil because he will hear you." The devil is simply a fallen angel who has power, but has no authority.

THE LORD REBUKE YOU

This phrase is very common to hear in many churches when the word devil is mentioned. It is very misused today. In the book of Jude we see it.

Jude 1:9 "YET MICHAEL THE ARCHANGEL, IN CONTENDING WITH THE DEVIL, WHEN HE DISPUTED ABOUT THE BODY OF MOSES, DARED NOT BRING AGAINST HIM A REVILING ACCUSATION, BUT SAID, THE LORD REBUKE YOU."

And just because the angel mentioned "The Lord rebuke you" all Christians also mention it.

The archangel Michael and the cherubim Lucifer (devil) are coercive forces and for that reason Michael did not dare to rebuke him. But God gave us the authority to do so. Jesus defeated the devil as a man, not as God.

The problem of the church is that it has not regained its authority in God; Authority that we lost since Adam sinned. As a result of that, the devil has taken away the identity of man. Man without identity does not even know who he is, where he comes from, where he is, or where he is going: speaking spiritually. That is why we believe that the angels are superior to us.

ANGELS OR DEMONS

We know that what are known as demons, are fallen angels. God did not create demons, He created angels. When they left their position they became demons.

Jude 1:6 "AND THE ANGELS WHO DID NOT KEEP THEIR PROPER DOMAIN, BUT LEFT THEIR OWN ABODE, HE HAS RESERVED IN EVERLASTING CHAINS UNDER DARKNESS FOR THE JUDGEMENT OF THE GREAT DAY;"

A demon is the one who leaves his position of authority. God had assigned a position to all angels, but as we know, Lucifer revealed himself to God and was thrown out of his assigned position and became a devil. This means that everything that gets out of its position of authority that God assigned, is a demonic influence.

EXAMPLE: If a son wants to control his father, he is coming out of his position of authority, therefore having a demonic influence. If a wife wants to control her husband, that is a demonic influence. If a leader in a church wants to control the pastor, that is a demonic influence.

REPENTED ANGELS

On one occasion, during a deliverance we found a repentant demon. The demon spoke through the mouth of the person we were delivering and said that he was an angel who guarded people from demons. At first, he surprised me with what he was saying. He said that he was one of the angels thrown from heaven because of what he had done but now he was one of those who is repented. I said, according to the word of God that could not be. He said: "Yes, I understand but I have a hope that He from above forgives me and that's why I help people," Making the story short, at the end we ordered him to leave and he started to cry and left. At the end of the deliverance, we asked the person if she was aware of the deliverance. She replied yes, and confirmed that sometimes she felt a presence in her bedroom but was not afraid.

In the experience I have of deliverance that can not be. Its simply a demon in the service of his master, the devil. Any order he gives, the demon has to obey it.

ANGELS WHO EXECUTE THE WORD

Angels are responsible for executing every word that comes out of your mouth. So be careful with the words you use.

Psalms 103:20 "BLESS THE LORD, YOU HIS ANGELS, WHO EXCEL IN STRENGTH, WHO DO HIS WORD, HEEDING THE VOICE OF HIS WORD."

As we can see in this text, the angels execute the word that comes from the mouth of God. But we also know that the Holy Spirit is in us and He who speaks through us. Now, if you use words of wickedness, demons are responsible for executing those words. If you mention words of blessing, the angels are in charge of executing those words. But if your angel is not activated nothing will happen.

ACTIVATE YOUR ANGEL

Demons do not need to be activated. They are already activated through the disobedience of man. On the other hand, your angel is bound, waiting for you to release him, or was assigned to another person, or to say it in some way: on vacation, but not working for you.

Through a prophetic act you may activate your angel. Act like you are untying someone, speak to your angel, and tell him that its time to get to work.

TESTIMONY

As I began to teach about the angels to the church we now pastor, I remember during a service, a demon manifested in a young woman. At that time we were starting to form a deliverance team and they took her to one of the rooms to be delivered. When I finished, I went to see what was happening with the deliverance; The demon who manifested had a legal right in the life of this young woman and did not want to leave. He had entered by her listening to metal rock music. She was screaming, kicking and making a scandal. Some grabbed her by the arms and others grabbed her feet. It was a show. Thank God that nothing like that happens anymore, because we have learned the position of authority. We give an order to the demons, they submit, and obey. Going back to the story, I told him to leave her alone so that the demon would be still. At that moment God allowed us to put into practice the teaching I was giving about the angels. One of the seers of the ministry saw an angel of deliverance enter the room. I told those in the room, "God is going to allow us to put into practice what we just learned" We gave the order to the angel to remove the demon, and all this is being observed through the seer in the spiritual realm . The seer begins to tell us what she sees: the angel took his sword and the demon began to resist, but he inserted his sword in the head of the young woman to cut off the demon's head. Instantly the young woman was free and the angel left.

Everyone, including myself were astonished. The young woman came to herself and we asked her how she felt. She said: "very light, but, I feel like a knife was inserted in my head." Surprised, we all looked at one another because it was exactly what the seer told us. We recheck it with what the young woman told us. That was the first time we experienced that the angels do what they are told. This means that if witches work with demons, the church must learn to work with the angels.

We personally know that God has assigned us three large angels. Everywhere we go, they go with us; the seers see them. God revealed it to a sister in dreams. We have seen proof because they have saved us from accidents.

One of the angels is in the form of a large eagle that covers the road on both sides. When it opens its wings, five hands come out from each wing and covers the car where we go.
On one occasion, doing a deliverance on a pastor, the demon of witchcraft manifested and spoke through his mouth. He told me that he wanted to kill me, but that he could not touch me or my pastors because the large angel did not allow him to even come close to us.

We have many testimonies like these. But what I want is for you to also live these angelic experiences in your life.

THE DEVIL IS ILLEGALLY ON EARTH

Psalms 115:16 "THE HEAVENS, EVEN THE HEAVENS, ARE THE LORD'S; BUT THE EARTH HE HAS GIVEN TO THE CHILDREN OF MEN."

This revelation will change your life regarding the devil. This text is saying that the heavens are of God and the earth is ours. God gave humans the earth. Therefore earth does not belong to the devil. The devil is illegally here on earth. For that reason, the devil needs a body in order to operate. That is why the devil needs humans in ignorance to use their bodies. Their body gives the devil authority to operate on the earth. He did with Adam and continues to do it till this day.

If the devil is an illegal and we are the legal ones on earth, who has authority over whom? The devil does not want humanity to realize these truths, because he operates in the ignorance of humanity.

CONCLUSION

I could continue to write much more about angels, but what I want is for you to believe these truths and activate your angel. Remember the devil and his demons are inferior to us and are also illegal upon the earth.

The time has come to take the devil and his demons out of our life, out of our home, our family, and our city.

Blessings.

Apostle Moises Ramirez

BIBLIOGRAPHY

— Study Bible. King James Version, review 1960.

— Thomson Reference Bible. King James Version Revision 1960. copied and written by Frank Charles Thomson D.D.,Ph. D.

— New International Version Study Bible

— New Living Translation Bible.

— Dr. Ana Mendez Ferrell. Iniquity, p.p.39- 51

— Dr. Ana Mendez Ferrell. Regions of Captivity www.VoiceOfTheLight.com

Apostle Moises Ramirez

Write to us at:

E220 Church
1241 Cypress St
Abilene, TX 79601

Telephone: 325.603.6230

Email: info@e220.church

Webpage: www.e220.church

facebook.com/E220church

47476395R00055

Made in the USA
San Bernardino, CA
01 April 2017